77 SURE-FIRE WAYS TO KILL A SOFTWARE PROJECT

Destructive Tactics That Cause Budget Overruns, Late Deliveries, and Massive Personnel Turnover

---

by

Daniel D. Ferry and Noelle Frances Ferry

Authors Choice Press

San Jose New York Lincoln Shanghai

77 Sure–Fire Ways to Kill a Software Project
Destructive Tactics That Cause Budget Overruns, Late Deliveries, and Massive
Personnel Turnover

Authors Choice Press
an imprint of iUniverse.com, Inc.

For information address:
iUniverse.com, Inc.
620 North 48th Street, Suite 201
Lincoln, NE 68504-3467
www.iuniverse.com

Originally published by Buy Books On the Web

ISBN: 0-595-12610-3

Printed in the United States of America

Dedication

To those countless software developers who wonder if their managers have any idea how to run a software project

CONTENTS

Preface

In 1988, after five years in preparation, the Federal Aviation Administration awarded IBM's Federal Systems Division a $2 billion contract to modernize hopelessly outdated air traffic control systems. The FAA heralded the Advanced Automation System (AAS) as the answer to crowded skies, long waits at airports, and overworked air traffic controllers. Without AAS, passenger and commercial flying would be unsafe by the year 2000.

IBM, surely one of the most respected and capable hardware and software companies in the business, assembled an impressive team. The principal subcontractor, Computer Sciences Corporation (CSC)—one of the largest software companies in the world, with an imposing number of civilian government and defense contracts—shared software development responsibilities for two million lines of code, while Raytheon Corporation—another highly regarded defense contractor—supported hardware development. To ensure that the delivered system would be exactly what controllers wanted and needed, both IBM and CSC put air traffic controllers on their payrolls. Mitre Corporation served as watchdog for the effort.

By 1994 the AAS program had missed several milestones and was severely over budget, but Loral Aerospace, a company careful with a dollar, had enough confidence in the continuation of the AAS program to purchase IBM Federal Systems and the contract.

1

Less than three months later the Federal Aviation Administration issued a stop work order and canceled the AAS program, citing cost and schedule overruns and poor software quality. Six hundred thousand lines of code were simply thrown away as 800 developers, managers, and support personnel scrambled to find new jobs.

Unlike AAS, most software projects in trouble are not canceled outright, and so publicly. They stumble along, missing milestones and spending far more than originally budgeted, and when they finally, mercifully end, managers proclaim victory, although the only opposition faced was self-generated.

77 Sure-Fire Ways to Kill a Software Project brings to light the reasons complex software projects consistently suffer budget overruns, late deliveries, and massive personnel turnover. However, instead of a dreary treatise, we present an irreverent, light-hearted look at the problem. We use the reverse thinking technique ("What could we do to really screw this up?") to demonstrate how management mistakes and blind reliance on methodology alienate developers and strangle progress.

Why We Wrote This Book

One of our friends recently commented that thirty years ago he derived so much pleasure doing software development that he would have paid the company to let him work. Now he drags himself into the office merely to put bread on the table. The first part of this remark is certainly an exaggeration, but the second part characterizes a crucial problem: software development has become increasingly more difficult and less enjoyable.

In 1969 we sat in cramped offices and programmed FORTRAN on punched cards, then submitted those card decks over the counter for compilation and execution, hoping for more than one run a day. Creating a new system from scratch took many months and many a long night of testing—but it was fun.

Today development computers are many times faster and more user-friendly. We can easily attain multiple compilations and runs in a morning. But creating a new system from scratch still takes many months and many a long night of testing—and it is painful.

We believe that the factors impeding higher productivity are the same factors that are making the job more difficult and less personally satisfying. We aim to educate developers and all levels of management to recognize the epidemic use of destructive management strategies, process improvement schemes, and development techniques. We have chosen to group these under the designation "tactics."

Many of these tactics were used, albeit infrequently, thirty years ago. Now, however, they are generally accepted as standard practice: winning the contract is everything— don't worry that the schedule is impossible; standardizing the development process is more important than the skill of the workers who develop the software; apply the waterfall model to all development; two new college graduates are more valuable than one forty-year old veteran; you can work employees long hours and then reward them with a pizza party . . . these tactics demotivate employees, cause projects to complete late and overbudget, and not infrequently result in project cancellation.

The software industry will probably never return to the pleasures of developing software thirty years ago, but if we can convince even a few top-level managers to change their ways, we will be successful.

Who Should Read This Book

Managers at All Levels

We demonstrate to managers—from first-line supervisors to the CEO—how their management tactics are impeding the progress of their projects and destroying the morale of their employees. If you are a manager, you fit into one of the categories listed below. What you can do to turn around your project depends on your management level and your willingness to change.

- Managers who may suspect these tactics are counter-productive but employ them anyway for some "important" reason (usually financial)

  - You are at a high level, such as vice president or program manager. You should read with an eye towards learning how you can avoid major problems and loss of talented personnel.

- Managers so impressed with their own management skills that they use these destructive tactics and to hell with their employees' welfare

  - *This book was written about you*, but you probably won't understand why.

- Managers who agonize about the project and strive to improve progress and the plight of the developers

  - You are employing destructive tactics only because upper management forces you to do so. You'll learn to recognize when destructive tactics are commanded and will finally understand why your employees are leaving at an alarming rate. Maybe, just maybe, you can convince upper management to change their ways.

Technical Leads and Developers

You'll learn to recognize bad management tactics, even though you won't be able to do anything about them. At your own level, you'll learn to avoid inadvisable design and implementation techniques, and thereby make your own jobs a lot easier and more fun.

A Note about Gender

Throughout the text we use "he, his, him" instead of "she, her, her" or "he/she, his/her, or him/her" purely for convenience. There is no implication that all bad managers are male. On the contrary, we have known quite a few bad female managers. When you read the tactics, feel free to envision your worst nightmare of a manager, whether that manager is male or female.

Introduction

So You Want to Kill a Software Project . . .

It takes a lot to kill a software project. Managers often induce partial failure with relatively little effort, but to achieve conclusive results, a clever manager will plan for disaster. Only skillful preparation, sound tactics, continuous monitoring, and process adaptation can bring about unqualified failure.

We will teach you the basics of killing a project. Instead of forcing you to rummage through the glut of software engineering texts to identify potentially damaging approaches, we'll equip you with 77 tactics proven on countless projects. Even if you have no experience as a manager, we will guide you through the confusing maze of possible courses of action and teach you how to virtually guarantee the failure of your project—all under the guise of ensuring quality, improving productivity, and maintaining morale.

No one tactic is sufficient to kill a project, but must be combined with others for full effect. Each project is unique, requiring a different set of tactics. Your job as a manager is to select the tactics appropriate to your project and combine them into an overall strategy that will ensure the desired result. This is where your skill as a manager comes into play. We can teach you the tactics, but only *you* can pick those which will be most effective on *your* project. Throughout the text we supply guidelines and suggestions, but in the end it is up to you to bring your project crashing to its knees.

What if you are already in the middle of a project? For example, if your team is already in the implementation phase, you're likely to have missed laying some of the groundwork for failure in the requirements and design phases. At this point it is difficult, but not impossible, to guarantee failure. Since every project undergoes requirements changes, you'll have the chance to go back and apply destructive tactics for new or modified requirements. In addition, the tactics in the management and morale sections can sabotage any phase of a project, regardless of prior project success.

However, by the time you read this, your project may have developed too much momentum towards success, and even your best efforts will not be enough to kill it. In that case, use whichever of the 77 tactics you can get away with, enjoy the resulting havoc, and vow to try harder when you plan subsequent projects. After all, next time you'll have us to guide you.

Chapter 1

Unhealthy Project Startups

The obvious time to begin destroying a project is before it is even in-house. If you're lucky enough to be in a position to influence which contracts your company will bid, then you can guarantee project failure from the start—and probably clinch your next promotion.

You've seen it happen again and again. A project comes in late and overbudget, and employees start a pool for which week the project manager will get the axe. Wrong. Upper management loves him and promotes him to the next level, where he can architect even greater disasters. Jealous, aren't you? Shouldn't this be your career plan?

To put you on the road to your next promotion, we'll teach you how to select a project particularly prone to failure, then precisely how to bid that project to set it up for the kill. Winning the contract will, of course, require you to hone your ability to look the contracting officer straight in the eye and lie without blinking. Once you've won the contract, this talent will come in handy for interviewing prospective employees. We'll guide you through the interview process, then show you how to saddle your new team with impossible schedules. It's really quite simple, and a lot of fun.

9

Tactic 1

Bid on Projects Requiring Unrealistic Schedules

Government contract officers often put out requests for puffery (RFPs) that specify impossible schedules. This is an old trick that everyone knows about and accepts without question. Your proper response is to bid the contract, promising on-time deliveries within budget. Since every other bidder does the same, you're all on an equal footing. Anyway, once you've won the contract, your company will make money regardless of schedule.

Developers like a challenge, so tell your team that the schedule is doable. Then go to your office, shut the door, and enjoy a good laugh.

Tactic 2

Buy a Failing Contract to Enter a New Arena

Sometimes it's necessary to buy a smaller, competing company working in a business arena you would like to enter. For example, if SmallCo currently has an Air Force software contract for radar systems protecting Outer Mongolia, and you want to expand into that playing field, buy SmallCo to get the contract. However, you have to be sure the contract is fixed price, not cost-plus-incentive.

Cost-plus contracts are for wimpy companies, whereas bidding a fixed price contract takes guts. On a fixed price contract you can be sure that the estimates of effort are way too low and that the chances of successful completion within budget are remote. In fact, you can be confident that SmallCo has already spent all the money, and you'll have to complete the contract on overhead.

With a fixed price contract, you're also proving to your client that your company has the vast corporate resources (VCR) and determination to tackle a tough job and do whatever it takes to complete that job on schedule. This "whatever it takes" philosophy creates challenges for your management team to develop ingenious cost-saving methods while attempting to drive developers to unattainable productivity levels.

11

Tactic 3

Make Sure Your Facility Fee Is Minimal

Bidding a low facility fee increases your chances of winning the contract, so take time to plan a workable approach to cut costs:

- House your employees in a cramped building. Assign more than two employees to an office, or, better yet, allot claustrophobic cubicles in an immense, poorly ventilated room.

- Rent a building within walking distance of the Okefenokee Swamp or some equally remote site with no public transportation. Your employees will no doubt complain—suggest carpooling.

- Make sure there are no restaurants in the area, This will encourage employees to work at their desks. Unfortunately, they'll expect to be paid for their lunch hours. Therefore, once the contract is underway, issue a proclamation that employees are required to be at work nine hours each day and *must* take a full hour for lunch.

- Pick a locale with a high incidence of crime. The presence of an undesirable element near the building will discourage employees from taking walks at lunch time or during breaks.

Tactic 4

Propose a Low Skill Mix

Bidding an RFP with the proper skill mix guarantees your company will lose the contract. Propose a low skill mix using the following guidelines:

- Anyone with four or five years of experience can be a first-line manager, even if he has never managed before.

- Developers with one or two years experience make good task leaders. Put them in charge of several IROCs (Idiots Right out of College) and demand peak results.

- Whenever possible, minimize the number of senior personnel with eight or more years experience. It just drives up the cost.

Tactic 5

Award the Proposal Team Important Management Slots

When you win the contract, your first step towards project failure is to establish your management team. Be careful not to pick managers who know how to plan, how to work out problems, and how to motivate people. Instead, choose your top managers from the proposal team.

The guys on the proposal team have been sitting around writing proposals for years without success. They're stale and their technical management skills are outdated, but now that they've lucked into a win, they'll want to be rewarded. Of course, anyone with real management skills is already out there managing, not working on proposals. By the way—putting these ne'er-do-wells on your management team will make the accountants happy, because senior management was running out of overhead charges for these losers.

Tactic 6

Staff from outside the Company

You should try to staff from outside the company. Ignore the fact that there are plenty of good employees in your company who would jump at the chance to work on a new project with new technologies. Many of these developers are over 40, and you probably need to get rid of them anyway to reduce labor costs (please see Tactic 74).

- Hire junior programmers fresh out of college to design the system. (see also Tactic 7)

- Staff your project with newcomers to the company who have no company loyalty and no concept of the company culture.

- Pay new employees higher salaries than your incumbent employees and conveniently leak this information.

- Give new employees the best equipment (powerful PCs, color X-terms) while the older, proven employees make do with IBM 3270 terminals and PCs from IBM's first shipment in 1982.

- Move new employees into window offices while relegating existing employees to interior offices, bullpens, or cubicles.

Tactic 7

Screen Candidates Mercilessly

If you followed Tactic 4, you bid a low skill-mix to win the contract. Now that you've won the contract, begin staffing as quickly as possible. Bring onboard your secret weapon—hordes of IROCs. Of course, you'll want to interview each candidate to ensure he has the minimum qualifications for your project:

- **Ability to think quickly***: Ask the candidate to spell "C", "C++", "IBM," "HTML," and "UNIX" (this is a tough one).

- **Creativity:** Ask to see the Internet home page the candidate created with an effortless web page editor. The ideal home page has pictures of the candidate's room, his sock drawer, and his most recent trip to Cleveland.

- **Knowledge of computer science:** Ask the candidate to describe a doubly-linked list and when it should be used. "Metal circles hooked together to keep my bike from being stolen" is an adequate answer.

- **Perseverance:** Ask the candidate to describe his toughest challenge. "A quarter keg with two buddies in four hours" is the kind of impressive achievement you're looking for.

- **Ability to get along with others:** Ask the candidate if he has any pets. Ferrets and rats are the preferred answer. If a candidate comes to the interview wearing more than three rats (live or dead), hire him on the spot.

16

- **Company Identification:** Any candidate who attends the interview in cutoffs or trousers with the crotch at his knees is prime material for your team.

- **Technical Ability (the most important qualification):** Give the candidate a programming test in which he has to add two numbers. Four or more pages of uncommented code is an appropriate solution.

Tactic 8

Pull SLOC Estimates from the Air

"SLOC" sounds like a monster from a grade-B movie or a popular TV series, but it stands for "Shifting Lines of Code." Another acronym for this is DSI (Dubious Source Instructions). As a project progresses, the estimated lines of code to be developed jumps astronomically from that originally anticipated, shrinks when the client becomes frightened, and increases as reality sets in, only to dwindle again when the client becomes cost-conscious. (This has no effect on the actual number of lines of code the project will finally generate.)

- Try to guess the magic KSLOC (Killer SLOC) number that the client has in his head. Don't worry about getting it correct—the client will inform you if you're wrong. You might want to use the latest software engineering methodology to determine the SLOC for each major function of the system: a SLOC dart board with a 20% higher estimate on each concentric circle until you reach the bullseye. Throw three times and average the results.

- Next, ask your team. They'll tell you, for example, that the project will take about 800 KSLOC. It's just a WAG (Wild-Assed Guess), but it'll make them feel good that you asked.

- The customer won't accept that number, but instead will (finally) inform you he thinks the number should be 600 KSLOC because that's all he has budget for.

- Tell your team to rework the numbers. They'll bitch and moan, then agree reluctantly that the project *might* be doable in 700 KSLOC.

- Go to the client and congratulate him—your staff agrees his estimate of 600 KSLOC is the right number.

Tactic 9

Stretch Those Hardware Dollars

A primary rule of project management is to give developers the hardware they need to do the job. But if you do that, they might actually complete it on time, within budget, regardless of the impossible schedule you've given them. Here are some ideas to ensure this doesn't happen:

- Install inefficient, low bandwidth communications lines throughout your building, and forget about buying uninterruptible power sources—they're too expensive.

- Put the target machine at the client site instead of in your building; install a single slow communications line between your building and the client site. Better yet, make it dialup.

- No matter what the capability of the target machine, give your team a development machine with only one-fourth the power and memory.

- Give your developers monochrome, line-oriented terminals the client has discarded. They'll bitch and moan, especially when they discover that the client has allocated top-of-the-line UNIX and Windows NT workstations to himself and his cohorts. These high-end machines will be used for reading all their personal e-mail and playing the latest computer games.

19

Tactic 10

Apply the Waterfall Model

Your government clients like the waterfall development model because it's easy to understand. It doesn't matter to them that the model has been abandoned by all sentient beings except federal government workers. Your client wants desperately to believe that you can nail down the requirements before design and that you can come up with a complete design before coding. He is quite nervous about the project—and rightly so. He needs stability, and the waterfall model gives it to him.

The waterfall model will also provide added amusement later, as your team struggles to put together design presentations without firm requirements and with only a vague idea of what the customer expects the system to accomplish.

Chapter 2

Development Mayhem

If you've followed our advice, you've won a contract for a failure-prone project, staffed it with incompetents, and set unattainable deadlines. Now it's time to start turning the technical screws.

Your first step is to force inadequate requirements on your team. That alone will take your project halfway to failure.

But you can't stop there. You have to keep up the pressure by making design decisions that will doom your project to later redesign. And you've got to stifle the design process with bad methodologies and tools that will make the design phase painful for your developers.

Eventually your battered team will have to implement that defective design. Unfortunately, at this point your team may make a comeback and start making real progress. We'll show you how to sabotage any recovery. At the end of this chapter you'll be an expert in tactics that will eat up your development time, overwhelm your budget, and intimidate your developers.

You're smiling, aren't you? You just can't wait to start playing. Read on and we'll all have a good laugh—well, not the developers, but who cares about them?

Tactic 11

Give Your Client That Warm, Fuzzy Feeling

To con your client into believing that you are actually interested in his ideas about how the system should work, hold regular, interminable meetings. Get someone to take copious notes and publish the minutes. This gives your client a warm, fuzzy feeling that your team knows what it's doing.

Document the requirements with some recognized methodology like structured analysis. Diagrams with lots of bubbles and arrows will always impress your client, even though he doesn't understand why there are so many bubbles or how the system fits together. That's OK. Neither do your developers.

Tactic 12

Leave Requirements Gaps and Discrepancies

Even your best system engineer can't ignore explicit requirements set forth by the client. "Produce images from the satellite data" is pretty explicit, and you have to make the client believe that your team is working toward that goal. However, wherever there is a question as to how the software should perform intermediate functions, you have an opportunity to create problems by leaving the requirements vague.

Another favorite is to write conflicting requirements. This is an art that only the best system engineers have mastered. Of course, it's easier to accomplish on a large project, where the system engineer claims to be the only person to understand all the requirements. With any luck, no one will realize the built-in discrepancies until integration or system testing.

Tactic 13

Begin Design While Requirements Are Fluid

Say you've got a client, who we'll call Mr. Code_Now, who wants you to start coding as soon as possible, with or without a design. He's from the old school, where programmers just jumped in and began coding in FORTRAN, and, if they were diligent, would document their code afterward with a few flowcharts.

Mr. Code_Now is already on your side, supporting your final goal. He expects you to start design work without solid requirements. If you want to make him really happy, start coding major portions of the system that are only vaguely understood by the system engineers, much less the programmers.

With this approach, you'll eventually have to redo the entire design, and if you're lucky, thousands of lines of code. This means more money in your company's pocket and a frustrated development team. Not too shabby.

Tactic 14

Pick a Fashionable Design Methodology

Structured, OO (object-oriented, a.k.a. obscure on-purpose), spiral, top-down, bottom-up, inside-out . . . the choice of a design methodology can be crucial to the success—or failure—of a project.

Your best plan would be to let each developer design in his or her own favorite method. This would lead to spaghetti code and lots of global variables. You should be so lucky. Generally, most clients are too smart to fall for this, and you'll have to follow some formalized methodology.

OK, choose some seductive methodology completely unfamiliar to your team, such as OOD (Object-Oriented Disaster). Hire a consultant to give a whirlwind (but incomprehensible) course. Then force all design work into that mold, whether or not the methodology is appropriate. You'll confuse your developers; you'll confuse your client; and best of all, you'll double or triple the amount of time necessary for the design phase.

Tactic 15

Generate Useless Design Products

Many clients, and even some managers, believe that CASE (Completely Autistic Software Engineering) tools will make design generation efficient and dependable. Let them. You know from experience that your developers can waste countless hours fitting their designs into something the tool will allow.

Many CASE tools produce structure charts and data dictionaries. Both products are of questionable (read "little") value, because they're obsolete as soon as coding begins. But they're great because they give your client that warm, fuzzy feeling and simultaneously use up precious development time. Structure charts are simple enough for most clients to understand (just lines and boxes, right?). Your developers will squander countless hours making these diagrams perfect. Then, when coding begins, and the diagrams and data dictionary are no longer up-to-date, make the developers go back and update them. Best to do this every build, so the developers end up applying fixes again and again.

To toughen your developers, put the CASE tool on a remote machine with a slow link to ensure 10- to 20-second response times to refresh the graphics—long enough to make developers grate their teeth in frustration, but not enough time for them to reach for something else to do.

Tactic 16

Keep the User Interface Design Ambiguous

Since the internals of your system are driven by the inputs and outputs, the proper design approach is to design the input and output subsystems first to check out external interfaces and to determine if the client and the operators like the GUI (Generally Useless Interface). Clearly you can't let that happen. It could shorten the development time considerably.

Accordingly, you must ignore the user interface as much as possible during development. Later, when the GUI is criticized by the client so that major changes are required, the associated design and code changes will domino throughout the system. You can always justify this decision to let the GUI slide by claiming

- Users don't know what they want, so why give them a choice?

- The user interface is straightforward and will be simple to develop.

- It's more important to design the guts of the system before the interfaces.

Tactic 17

Require Abundant Attendance at Inspections

If you take the time to look in the literature (and you really should, if only to avoid possible productivity-enhancing ideas), the methodology that has proven most effective in improving the quality of software is the mandatory use of design and code inspections. To create havoc on your project, you might try to do away with inspections, but upper management would probably not permit this—inspections are an important step towards earning the SEI (Software Exhibition Institute) Level 3 appraisal.

Assuming you have to utilize inspections, how can you minimize their effectiveness?

- Require mobs of developers to attend every inspection. We're talking here about people with only a peripheral interest, not the moderator, chief inspector, author, and the system engineer. If you can tie up ten people for two hours (the normal maximum allowable inspection duration), you've shot half a staff week.

- Require anyone who might conceivably use the code to be at the inspection, even if this unit is completely hidden from their code.

- Invite one or two "experts" who will eat up time arguing about the most elegant approach to solve the problem. This approach works particularly well for reuse components (see Tactic 20).

Tactic 18

Make Developers Fight for Every Purchase

Whenever one of your developers wants to buy some software productivity tool (like a compiler), make him jump through hoops to justify the expenditure. The effort required of this would-be purchaser should be proportional to the cost of the tool except for very inexpensive tools. For any tool that costs less than $1000, you should make the developer download a trial version and spend enormous amounts of time preparing a demonstration to prove its worth.

Tactic 19

Get Technically Involved

You're not supposed to attend inspections, but you can get around this sacred rule by assigning yourself some development work to justify your attendance. This will, of course, intimidate the author of the inspection, who doesn't want to look bad in front of you, his manager:

- Instead of just determining the problems with the design or code and letting the inspection author resolve the problem off-line, make your team solve the problem immediately. This will waste time that could be spent more effectively looking at the rest of the inspection material.

- Force your ideas on the team. After all, you're their manager, and you should have the last say.

- After hours, when all your developers have left, get onto the system (you have root password and access to your developers' directories) and change any design or code you don't like. And who of your developers is going to be brave enough to tell you where to get off?

Tactic 20

Design Reusable Units by Committee

For the moment let's not get into the argument about whether or not your project should try to employ reusable code. We'll return to that seductive question in Tactic 32. Instead, let's assume that you've made the decision to implement reusable components and are now faced with the perplexing question of how to actually do it.

Most packages (Ada-ese and Java-ese) and classes (C++-ese and Java-ese) are best designed by one person who has a coherent idea of what the package or class is supposed to do. Champions of reusable components, however, feel compelled to assemble a large group to design even the simplest component. This approach has definite advantages for the would-be project-killer:

• It consumes inordinate amounts of time in design and code inspections.

• Disagreements among developers over stylistic issues often lead to bad feelings and poor morale.

• The person with the original idea (and the only one who understands it!) leaves the project just as the reusable component hits the street.

Tactic 21

Don't Bother with COTS Software

Never purchase COTS (Constantly Ordering the Sequel) software if you're trying to drive up the cost of a project. Whenever possible, apply the not-invented-here (NIH) rule: if it would be cheaper, more efficient, and easier to buy a COTS product, you should make the developers build it instead.

For example, when faced with the task of saving various items of information needed later in the processing by several subsystems, many of your developers will want to use a COTS relational database. Your response should be "No, way, José." Make them write their own database system. The result of this proclamation will be a mad scramble among the software theoreticians on the project to develop a reusable database component. By the time the dust settles, you'll have spent three or four times what a COTS database would have cost, and everyone will be dissatisfied with the result. Congratulations on a job well done.

Tactic 22

Make Unit Designs Resemble Code

Ultra-detailed design is a particular favorite of managers who believe that designers are designers and coders are coders. Require your developers to produce PDL (Program Divining Language) so detailed that it would be easier to write the code. This extends the design phase and squanders precious time your team should be devoting to coding. During implementation, when the design has changed again and again (as it always does), you'll look back on this phase of the project and smile contentedly.

An added benefit of this tactic is that the coder has no idea of the rationale behind the code, and so will have no way to fix the code when it breaks. Let's look at an example of how this can be done.

Understandable PDL that you should *discourage*:

```
Move the last two data items to the beginning of the
    buffer
```

Detailed PDL that you should *encourage* (emphasize that NO comments are necessary to understand this design):

```
Move Buffer_A.Field_B.Subfield_C[Some_Pointer -2]
    to Buffer_A.Field_B.Subfield_C[0]
Move Buffer_A.Field_B.Subfield_C[Some_Pointer -1]
    to Buffer_A.Field_B.Subfield_C[1]
```

Tactic 23

Give Spice to the Design with Asynchronous Processes

The lure of multiprocessing is irresistible to the average programmer. He'll mask his inability to produce a workable serial design by producing a design complicated with asynchronous processes—a design intended to wow management and the client. (It doesn't matter that the target platform has only one processor, so that asynchronous processes won't provide any additional speed.) Let it be common knowledge that

- You expect to see subsystem designs overflowing with asynchronous processes.

- Single process subsystems are inefficient and will be challenged at design inspections.

- The single-processor target machines will eventually be replaced with multi-processor machines. (This is an outright lie, but who cares?)

Tactic 24

Create Lots of Clever New Types

At the beginning of design, proclaim that all built-in types (e.g., integer, Boolean, short, long, float, string) are too vague for the project. Redefine all standard types to guarantee that the code can be ported to other platforms with different built-in type definitions (even if the chances of this port happening are as remote as the nearest pulsar).

Whenever possible, define these types to be inconsistent with the built-in base types. This will result in serious performance problems, not to mention all the swearing and hair pulling that developers will go through trying to match up incompatible types.

Tactic 25

Encourage Designers to Use Complicated Data Structures

Following closely on the confusion generated by Tactic 24, this tactic will generate massive consternation among developers:

- Base new types on the incompatible types from Tactic 24.

- Continue nesting types to three, four, or five layers. This works best if the nested types reside in separate files in different directories so developers have to search for them.

- Promote the use of every data structure that the developers learned in Computer Science 201.

Given half a chance, the average programmer will store four related variables in a doubly-linked list nested inside an array, which in turn is nested in a stack or queue, depending on which one is the programmer's favorite data structure. Aside from the obvious performance problems, this approach will require complicated loops and decision logic with lots of juicy pointers. The probability of nasty coding mistakes is 100%.

Tactic 26

Advocate the Use of Side Effects

When you turn on the windshield wipers in your car, does the hood pop open or the radio come on? Probably not. You wouldn't buy a car like that, and any automotive engineer who designed side effects like that would soon be looking for another job. No so with software developers. Software developers see nothing wrong with setting unrelated global variables, clearing buffers, and nulling important pointers whenever the operator decides to check the system time.

This works *for* you. Encourage the developers to use the two basic types of side effects:

- The "Oh, crap. I forgot about that thing over there" side effect: This occurs after the developer has generated a design that he loves, but has found one or more (probably *many*) small glitches that need to be taken care of. Instead of stepping back and redesigning, he throws in a side effect for each glitch.

- The "I need job security" side effect: This side effect is inserted for the sole purpose of making the developer indispensable to the project. Because of the intricate weaving (spaghetti code) of the design, only he can understand the code. If he is ever let go, he has the satisfaction of knowing no one else has any idea how the code works.

Tactic 27

Establish Exhaustive Naming Conventions

Nothing will drive your developers up the wall so quickly as bizarre naming conventions for units, data structures, global variables, arguments, even variables local to a procedure.

Units: Require absurd abbreviations within the name.
Example:

>   Use   Utl_sbi_Rd
>   NOT   Utility_StreamBufferedInputRead

Arguments: Preface these with the subsystem abbreviation or acronym, then append "Arg" to irritate the programmers smart enough to determine that these variables are arguments. If you restrict the total number of characters in all names to an arbitrarily small number, the required prefixes and suffixes will minimize the number of characters that could give the maintenance programmer any clue to the purpose of the variable.
Example:

>   Use   Utl_Var_IS_Arg
>   NOT   InputString

Local Variables: There is no possible justification for requiring local variables to follow naming conventions, so this will make programmers furious!
Example:

>   Use   Utl_TokCnt_LocVar
>   NOT   TokenCount

Tactic 28

Concentrate on Cosmetics, Not Functionality at Inspections

One of the cleverest tricks you can pull is to have inspectors concentrate on trivialities: spelling, spacing, indenting, capitalization of words in comments/PDL; format of the prologue; and grammar. Require comments to be full sentences! Since inspections are generally limited to two hours (spectator inspectors go to sleep after one hour), waste that first hour by getting all the trivial comments out of the way.

The PAO (Project Aggravation Office) will be your staunchest supporter in this move. Their personnel are experts at worrying about trivial items and ignoring meaty problems. By concentrating on trivia, your developers will not have time during the inspections to review the design or code for thoroughness, accuracy, and efficiency.

Tactic 29

Plan Each Build at the Last Minute

This tactic assumes your code development is taking place in multiple four- to five-month builds instead of one massive, two-year effort that begins at CDR (Comical Design Review) and ends when you throw the software over the fence to System Test and run like hell. Builds generally make code development more efficient by focusing efforts on smaller, more manageable chunks of the system. You can partially neutralize this gain by forcing your managers and tech leads to ignore the upcoming build until the previous one has been completed:

- Apply pressure to "get this build done right," even though it's only the first of seven builds.

- Hold twice-daily status meetings for the last month of the build and require professional looking slides from your leads (see Tactic 47).

- Keep leads busy writing reports (see Tactic 53).

- Authorize vacations for key personnel during the last weeks of the build and the first weeks of the upcoming build.

- Try to keep everyone totally confused about what work they should be doing for the upcoming build.

Tactic 30

Declare System Administration a Part-Time Job

Your client wonders what your system administrators are doing all the time—probably just sitting around for hours playing solitaire, Battleship, and other mind-numbing games on their envied high-end workstations. Accordingly, you can easily convince the client that you will save him a lot of money by making the system administrator work as a developer at least half-time.

Be sure the system administrator gets the message that he has to complete his development work on time. Also tell him his system administration duties are his highest priority, except for his development work. This ambiguous statement of priorities should confuse him completely and allow you to berate him for missing development milestones and for failing to support the system appropriately.

With any luck, the system administrator will quit and you'll have to hire a new system administrator at a higher salary. Then play the same game with him.

Tactic 31

Modify Common Code Frequently

How can you make your CM (Chaos Management) group torment your developers? The best way to accomplish this is to create a few low-level code units referenced by the hierarchy of all other units in the system. A good example of this would be a unit that contains all the numbers associated with messages exchanged by the subsystems. All you have to do is add one or two new messages per week (inserted into the middle of the list, of course) so that CM will have to rebuild common code. The rebuild will take them two days, and with just one clever decision you'll waste 40% of the development time every week.

A further refinement of this tactic is to complain that your development team is not moving forward fast enough and that they should be coming in on weekends to catch up.

Tactic 32

Require Developers to Employ Reusable Software

If you followed Tactic 20, you now have a library of reuse components developed by committee. These components

- Require triple the normal development time,
- Have complicated interfaces that no one except the original programmer can understand,
- Utilize multiple layers of objects, resulting in poor performance.

Now force your developers to use these components. Nothing is so irritating to a developer as being coerced to accept someone else's code when he knows that code is complicated and inefficient. Developers will especially protest when they have to pervert their original designs to shoehorn in the reuse components.

Eventually, someone in System Test will discover that the reuse components consume way too much CPU and memory resources. Each participating group will then gladly dump the reuse components and code their own subsystem-specific versions, reverting to the original, clean designs they had to change to shoehorn in the reuse components.

You can waste hundreds of staff hours developing these reuse components just to throw them away. Be sure to advertise the success of the reuse group and give the reuse manager a big bonus.

Tactic 33

Forego Prototyping

Any system that is the least bit complicated has unique hardware components or software schemes that have not been tried before.

If you delight in watching uncertainty and panic cross the faces of your developers, approve the use of these components and schemes without prototyping. Justify your decision by claims that you are saving the client money that would be wasted on the throwaway prototypes. If you're lucky, your team will have to discard and redo a large portion of the design because the hardware didn't work as planned or the software scheme had inherent, unforeseen flaws.

Tactic 34

Don't Plan for Large-Scale Debugging

Your developers assume they'll be able to use their IDE (Impractical Development Environment) debuggers for integration and system test just as they did for unit and subsystem testing. Great! In those larger environments, IDE debuggers are more difficult to use, especially if the subsystems are separately executing and synchronized processes. That means debugging will take many times longer than it should. Various solutions to this problem are possible, and you have to guard against your team using them:

- Don't purchase special software tools that instrument the code to permit real-time debugging. If a group wants to buy such a tool, make them first try to prove to you that the tool is cost-effective—proof you will never accept.

- Don't let developers embed conditional print statements in the code. After all, that would cause performance problems, right?

- Don't let developers embed compile-guarded print statements in the code. Just say they'll be useless because you'd have to recompile (sure it's ludicrous, but who cares?).

Tactic 35

Make It Fast

"You can always make a working program faster, but you can't always make a fast program work" is a belief that you have to drum out of your developers.

Your client will always support your contention that the system has to be designed for speed from the very beginning. Hang signs all over your development area that say *Code for speed!*, *Speed first!*, **and** *Fast code makes a happy client!* Give impressive awards to developers who write fast, unmaintainable code.

Whenever one of these superprogrammers leaves, assign someone to take over the orphaned code. When the stuckee informs you that superprogrammer's code will have to be rewritten to make it maintainable, make a big show of reluctantly agreeing to this schedule hit, then tell the stuckee that he has to make the code twice as fast as the old code.

Tactic 36

Require Exhausting Unit Testing

Let's have a quiz. First cover the answers at the bottom of the page. You get 5 points for each correct answer:

1. How much unit testing is enough?

2. Which type of unit testing should be performed?

3. Give an example of the type of test that should be included in a white box unit test matrix.

4. When should you require unit testing? (hint: two-part answer, each 5 points)

Scoring:

20-25 points: Good job.

10-15 points: You need some help identifying what is important to your project.

Below 10 points: You may not be mean enough to profit from this book.

Answers:

1. There can never be enough unit testing, but it should at a minimum severely impact your schedule and cause developers to work into the wee hours of the morning.

2. White box: it takes more time and produces the least payback. White box testing verifies not that the unit does what it is supposed to do, but that the compiler works. (Black box testing, on the other hand, tests a unit's functionality. This makes sense, so right away you'll have to rule it out.)

3. Verify the unit's ability to handle the moon falling into the earth (only 30 million years in the future!). Any answer similarly farfetched is correct.

4. Require white box unit testing when the unit is (1) *first coded* and (2) *whenever it is changed* as a consequence of subsystem, integration, or system testing. It doesn't matter that only one line has changed—a line is a line.

Tactic 37

Dictate Rigorous Verification of Unit Test Results

Another trick to making unit testing difficult and time consuming is to require unit test drivers and test results verification:

- Make your team develop unique standalone drivers to test each unit—this will double the number of units your team has to code.

- Don't allow a unit to be incorporated into the subsystem until its test results have been verified. This will shake up the subsystem test schedule nicely.

- Make one person in each group (probably the subsystem tech lead) review standalone driver code and white box testing results—this will cause a bottleneck as the tech lead becomes inundated with reams of paper that he has no time to look at, much less validate.

Tactic 38

Don't Plan for Integration Testing

You know that the subsystems have little chance of fitting together properly for integration testing, regardless of voluminous documents, countless inspections, and extensive subsystem testing. However, you have to convince your client that no effort is necessary for all this disparate code to easily dovetail into a workable system. This is what he wants to hear:

- Appropriate test data sets will be available when needed.

- Hardware resources will free up just at the right time for integration testing.

- The integration test plan can be cobbled together from subsystem test plans.

- CM of the code given to the integration team will be a trivial process.

- Subsystem personnel will have plenty of time to help with integration testing while they're planning the next build.

- All subsystems will be ready to test at one time, so you won't need any software to simulate interfaces.

Tactic 39

Assign the Wrong Person to Do Integration Testing

The cleverest way to mess up integration testing is to choose an integration team lead who is completely incompetent. Choose someone who

- Is a die-hard FORTRAN programmer on DEC VAX or IBM mainframe although your project is a C/C++ system on UNIX (or vice versa).

- Has been a manager for several years but likes to boast about what a great coder he was.

- Is known for never checking his e-mail.

- Continually spouts off about his lack of dedication to the company and the project.

- Spends most of his day walking the halls complaining to other discontented incompetents.

- Has no knowledge of what the system is supposed to do.

- Will in the near future be brought up on sexual harassment charges.

Tactic 40

Perform Big Bang Testing

Tell the managers to deliver their subsystems to the integration team one week before you toss the software to System Test. Be careful. If you tell them to deliver to integration one month before the System Test toss, the additional pressure might actually make them produce earlier. With a one-week pre-integration deadline, the subsystems will deliver on a bell curve schedule:

- Your best subsystem will deliver two weeks early. Consider splitting up this efficient team and introducing some real do-nothings into the group.

- Most subsystems will deliver a few days late, resulting in a two-day integration.

- Your worst subsystem will deliver two weeks *after* the date for delivery to System Test. This means that integration tests cannot be performed with this subsystem, and some workaround will have to be found.

No substantive integration testing can be performed in this short period, even if the integration team works round-the-clock, so System Test better watch out when you throw your software over the fence, because it will really hurt when it hits.

Tactic 41

Give Everyone Beepers

What do you do when System Test personnel begin to identify problems with your team's code?

- Stall as long as possible!
    - Tell System test to go back and do every test a second time because you don't believe them.
    - Require extensive paperwork and approvals at all levels before you let your team attack the problems.
- When you can stall no longer . . .
    - Start putting pressure on your team to resolve the problems immediately. Let everyone in your team know that they are expected to work round-the-clock without extra pay to fix these problems that are, by all rights, their fault anyway.
    - Give everyone on the team beepers so that even cosmetic problems discovered in the middle of the night can be communicated to them and resolved without delay.

It doesn't matter that the software is not life-critical software or that the final delivery date is months away; Burn your people out NOW so they won't have any residual energy or commitment later, when real problems begin to surface.

Tactic 42

Let Your Team Make Changes on the Fly

Let your developers deliver local copies of code fixes. Then turn your back when they fail to update the unit in your CM libraries. With all the pressure you're applying for them to work into the middle of the night, they want to get the fix—any fix—out the door and into the hands of System Test.

You won't see the full benefit of this tactic until the next build, when unconfigured code changes result in System Test once again writing problem reports on many of the same problems from the previous build.

Chapter 3

Management Tricks to Guarantee Your Project Will Be Late and Overbudget

What can you do when your project appears to be heading for success and your client is thrilled by your progress? This *is* an unlikely situation, but every project has some minor successes, and you'll have to guard against that possibility, no matter how remote. Instead of waiting for these (hopefully minor) successes to occur, you must institute a first-strike strategy.

Probably the most effective first-strike strategy is to have your team produce at least one printed page of documentation for every executable line of code. We'll give you specific tactics to implement this approach on any contract, but you'll easily double this metric on Federal government contracts as a consequence of day-to-day paperwork and deliverable documents.

Your QA (Quantity Assurance) team members are your best conspirators when trying to kill productivity because they are experts in binary arithmetic and counting. They can tell you whether or not a project has produced a specific product, or give you a list of all defects found in your standards and procedures. However, ask them about the quality of the software your team is producing and they'll stare at you like deer caught in the headlights. This all works to your advantage.

Rather than ensure a good product, QA will constantly count check marks and bother your developers to buy into various types of process improvement (e.g., SEI, CMM, TQM, and ISO9000).

The hype for process improvement is tremendous because software engineering is a particularly fertile field for hype. Consider the current darling of the masses, the object-oriented language Java, which is mediocre but has an extravagant marketing campaign. Over 200 half-baked books have been written about it. Eureka, we've got an instant, if questionable, winner. (Ada probably could have been a contender, but the marketing campaign stunk.)

When you combine process improvement hype with international standards organizations and government decrees, you find top-level managers scurrying around trying to raise their organizations to increasingly ludicrous notions of process achievement. Absolutely *nothing* is more exciting to upper management (mid-level managers know better) than the words "process improvement," so you won't have any trouble convincing corporate to join in this lunacy.

The merit of these initiatives to you is the almost unbelievable amount of time that can be wasted—time that could have been used to produce a better product instead of a better process.

It doesn't get any better than this.

Tactic 43

Let System Engineering Slip Milestones

Halfway through the implementation phase System Engineering will still be adding new requirements and changing the old ones. This is a direct result of System Engineering personnel being confused about what the system is supposed to do. You can thank your excellent staffing plan for this situation. And remember the Waterfall Model? Really worked well, didn't it?

System Engineering managers will blithely promise to have the requirements additions and modifications completed just in time for the next build, but everyone knows they are lying. The software teams, on the other hand, have been working with the old requirements. With new requirements promising major changes, software development is at a standstill. Your software managers will therefore try to slip their own schedules whenever System Engineering is late.

DON'T LET THEM DO THIS! Tell them they have to absorb any System Engineering slips, and make them commit to completing the build on time, regardless of whether they have requirements. System Engineering will eventually throw together some incredibly useless and contradictory requirements by the middle of the build, and your developers will be forced to make an heroic effort to finish the build on schedule.

Tactic 44

Welcome Creeping Requirements, Especially During Coding

Particularly insidious requirements changes are those that grow out of discussions that you and your predecessors have conducted with the client. These incremental requirements are sometimes called feature creep, because, although each additional feature is small, their collective impact on your schedule can be staggering. Statements from the client on why you should include these requirements free of charge generally contain certain phrases designed to disarm any opposition:

- "Everyone agreed to this a long time ago." (You'd be a jerk to say no.)
- "These changes are all well-known and documented." (Fat chance)
- "This is just a minor change, so you should absorb it." (Major effort)
- "This is derived from the requirement to . . ." (Completely unrelated to . . .)
- "These are corrections, so we have to do them." (Whose mistake was it anyway?)
- "You said you could do it." (Feasibility implies obligation)

Creeping requirements are a godsend. You can simultaneously blow your budget, blow your schedule, and burn out your developers by accepting any and all creeping requirements.

Tactic 45

Do Lots of Presentations

It looks like your team may be able to pull it off. They have a tight schedule, but they're motivated and solving major problems. What can you do to stop this headlong rush to success?

One answer, a particular favorite on Federal government contracts, is to stop all work to prove that you're doing work—in other words, do a presentation. The supposed goal of presentations is to get concurrence from your client on the requirements and design. In truth, your client understands little of the technical content of the following presentations, but he longs for that warm feeling that your team knows what it's doing:

- SRR (Senseless Requirements Review) — ensures that no one agrees what the system should do.

- PDR (Preliminary Disaster Review) — proves that your team understands the current requirements (which will change completely by the time the project is over) and that they're really scared they won't have enough time to finish the work.

- CDR (Comical Design Review) — unveils a design so vague that no one could code it or so detailed that everyone will wonder why you didn't.

- BDR (Build Disaster Review) — guarantees that you know how impossible and unpleasant the build will be before you start.

Tactic 46

Make Everyone Stop Development to Update Documentation

If everything is running smoothly, it's time to stop the headlong rush to success by documenting the development effort (see also Tactic 45). You can justify this approach as follows:

- "What if everyone left the project?" (Really, when have you ever seen your whole staff vacate like programmers deserting a sinking project?)

- "We have to have a baseline." (The baseline is really the engineering drawings and the code, not some entirely useless diagrams that the developers only drew to impress the client.)

The worthwhile lifetime of a software document depends on where you are in development. For example, the SRS (Senseless Requirements Specification) has little relevance after preliminary design has been completed. Why not waste valuable development time updating it, especially since you've got all these new and changed requirements? While you're at it, make your teams update the PDS (Preliminary Disaster Specification), and the DDS (Detailed Disaster Specification) while they are coding. This can consume inordinate amounts of developers' time for weeks, even months. Your programmers will hate you for this, but your client will love you for it. See also Tactic 15.

Tactic 47

Schedule as Many Meetings as Possible

Need another excellent time waster? How about an assortment of useless meetings?

- Process Improvement (SEI, CMM, TQM, ISO9000) meetings — their uselessness is well-documented.

- Department meetings — At least every other week have your managers get their teams together to tout the blessings of process improvement and changes to company policies.

- Project level meetings — Every week you should drag your subsystem tech leads to a meeting with the client to defend their status and to review, in gruesome detail, all requirements and design changes, especially those incorporated last year but never formally approved.

- Staff meetings — Make your managers attend your staff meeting, where once again they'll be required to defend their schedule slips and discuss the same requirements and design changes reviewed at the project-level meetings.

- Daily integration meetings — No other meeting is so intimidating to your managers and their tech leads as the daily integration meeting:

  - Always hold integration meetings even if the development is going well (perish the thought). Maybe you can waste enough time to change that rosy picture.

  - Hold meetings at 7:00 AM and 6:00 PM to thoroughly demoralize and fatigue your managers and leads.

  - These meetings work better and are more humiliating when your teams are late, overworked, and exhausted.

-   Require your managers to present their status using elaborate overhead transparencies.

-   Gloat as your managers and leads try desperately to prove their teams are actually making progress, no matter how minuscule.

Tactic 48

Require Formal Intermediate Deliveries

Normally you would only have your team deliver the software to your client at the end of one of the later builds, after most of the problems are worked out. However, if your teams are rolling too fast, slow them down by requiring formal deliveries of intermediate software products. Do this a couple times during each build to kill their productivity and cripple their momentum. In each of these formal deliveries,

- Generate delivery documents that list all units and reasons for their inclusion/omission in the delivery (added/changed/deleted), along with any references to fixing past problems.

- Prepare a mini-presentation for the client (with no less than 25 or 30 overhead transparencies) that recounts details of the subsystem's requirements and design.

- Route all delivery products through the PAO rep, who will, of course, reject the delivery because of various small discrepancies that will not affect functionality or performance.

Tactic 49

Punish Teams Meeting Their Schedule

Sometimes you have a good team that significantly outperforms its peers. Punish them in one or more of the following ways:

- Make the good team do extra, tedious work, such as preparing the delivery documents.

- Loan out members of the good team to bolster less efficient teams. Be sure to let the receiving team members know you don't think much of their abilities!

- Split up the good team and replace the efficient developers with lousy ones.

- If splitting up the team would be too obvious, assign some ne'er-do-wells to the team. They'll bring down the overall quality and productivity by consuming the good team members' time and energy.

Tactic 50

Change the Development Environment

What if coding and testing are cruising along without major mishaps? Is there some simple way mess to up the schedule? The resounding answer is "YES!" Simply change the development environment in any of the following ways, ordered from least impact to greatest impact:

- Upgrade the operating system or the COTS database management system.

  - Your team will need anywhere from one day to two weeks to recover.

- Declare that all code should meet ANSI standards or be POSIX-compliant.

  - The resulting incompatibilities in the code will require several weeks to resolve (recoding and retesting).

- Turn on "full optimization" in the compiler flags.

  - The stablest code in your subsystems will fail to generate the same results as the day before the change.

  - It's entirely possible that your software may never recover from this change, and you will have to drop back to less optimization or no optimization. But you've perturbed the project, so the exercise was a success.

- Switch operating systems from MVS to UNIX or vice-versa.

  - A fantastic idea! This will set you back at least one full build.

Tactic 51

Promise the Client Anything

We've previously discussed your client's lack of knowledge and failure to understand the system design. Based on this knowledge deficit, the client will typically ask your team to develop useless tools, to deliver early, or to support special tests with interfacing systems.

Promise your client anything he wants, regardless of the screams of outrage and predictions of doom from your software teams. Whether or not you deliver on any of these promises is immaterial. Presidential candidates and corporate executives have been playing this game for years. If you want to play the game, you've got to learn to play like the big boys.

Tactic 52

Don't Worry the Client by Presenting the True Status

Since the client has no idea what your team is developing, but wants desperately to maintain that warm, fuzzy feeling, it would seem silly to burden him with the truth.

You're going to deliver the system two or three months late. Why worry the client until the last minute?

- A week before the delivery date, drop a few hints to the client that your team may be a day late. That's an acceptable slippage, and the client will be impressed that you have the schedule planned almost to the hour.

- On the day before delivery (or even on the very day of delivery if you have the guts!) tell the client that your team will be at least two to three weeks late, and possibly a month or more. Act as baffled as your client.

- When that prediction turns into two, then three months, the client will thank you for not worrying him early in the development.

Tactic 53

Keep Subsystem Leads Busy Writing Reports

Towards the end of a build, your subsystem leads have little time to do anything but work with their teams in a last ditch attempt to complete the build. That situation offers an excellent opportunity to inundate the leads with the responsibility for producing numerous reports. Focus the leads' thoughts and energy on paperwork instead of on software. Every piece of paper you force out of a subsystem lead equates to several hours he could have spent on his subsystem:

• Written status reports (with overhead transparencies) presented at the daily status meetings.

• Weekly and monthly progress reports in three different flavors
  – Truthful versions for the project manager
  – The same reports sanitized for the client
  – Presentation slides for meetings with the client

• Subcontractor evaluations: You can make your leads rework these again and again to justify giving negative or positive ratings. Eventually the leads will give up out of frustration and resort to mediocre, vanilla ratings every month.

• Process improvement success stories. (These, of course, are bald-faced lies.)

• Newsletter articles praising the development effort.

• Pop-up staffing and budget analyses for the next five years. Be sure to always make the due date for a pop-up report at least one week earlier than the date you request it from the leads.

Tactic 54

Don't Use Technical Editors or Word Processing Experts

Your developers are earning somewhere between $15 (entry level) and $50 (top leads) an hour. Most of them are also appalling spellers and dreadful typists (maybe one in five hundred can touch-type with more than two fingers). It follows then that a wise manager would leave the generation of rough drafts of technical documents to the developers and get technical editors and word processing experts to honcho and clean up the final documents.

No. No. No.

- Make your developers learn whatever word processing program is in vogue with the client and painstakingly produce those final versions of the documents.

- Explain to the client that technical publications department charges are way out of line, and that he'll save money if you have the developers do the pubs work.

- Your developers will be forced to work extra hours (but they're free hours, aren't they?) to do both the documentation and their development work. Boo hoo.

Tactic 55

Assume the Lowest Common Denominator

The bell curve of the normal distribution applies to any profession from serial killers to postal workers to software developers (no evolutionary scale or resemblance implied). The software engineering solution to the varying capabilities of developers is to assume they are all near the low end of the bell curve, at a point called the LCD (Least Capable Developer, sometimes Logic-Challenged Developer). QA will gladly help you hamstring your top developers and shepherd the marginally competent ones:

- Establish excruciatingly cumbersome standards and procedures that allow no leeway for creativity: standard naming conventions (see Tactic 27), design and coding guidelines (see Tactic 15), design inspections, code inspections, SENs (Software Engineering Nostrums)—all the trappings of modern software engineering.

- Hold periodic (at least monthly) audits to verify that the developers are following the standards and procedures to the letter.

- Punish transgressors by making them

  - Correct the deficiencies in their process

  - Write an action plan to show how they will prevent such dereliction in the future

  - Participate in the next audit

Tactic 56

Require Developers to Meet Inspection Metrics

The appropriate number of major defects, N, that should be found in an inspection is as important to QA as prime numbers are to a mathematician or magic numbers to a nuclear physicist. The story goes that over a period of many years QA personnel have been correlating inspection statistics to the quality of software (kind of reminds you of monks in the Middle Ages poring over forgotten manuscripts), and they've finally decided that the value of N is 10. How did they *really* arrive at this number?

- 15 major defects in an inspection is obviously too many. It indicates that the author of the design or code is incompetent.

- 5 major defects seems a little low. Clearly the inspection team didn't work hard enough to find all the errors.

- N = (5 + 15)/2 = 10

You can use this number to torture your developers. If most inspections don't have 10 ± 2 major defects, QA will write a report to you that developers are incompetent designers, coders, and inspectors. When you get these reports, come down hard on your team. They'll counter by inventing major errors when they review good design/code and, by tacit agreement, ignore many major errors in bad code.

Tactic 57

Require Formal Inspections for All Code Changes

A normal, healthy software engineering approach is to assume that code changes during testing correct problems, and to believe the test results, but who said we're trying to be healthy here? Inspections take a lot of work, especially if you make the developers create ten copies of pretty-printed inspection packages, send them out four days before the inspection, and hold a formal meeting. This is fine, but if your goal is to maximize the depletion of development time, then requiring multiple inspections and regression testing will go a long way towards advancing that goal. Require reinspections and regression testing if there are any changes during

- Unit testing — especially if the developer used print statements and then removed them. Any modifications, even cosmetic, should force the developer to reexecute unit tests.

- Subsystem testing — Modifications require reexecuting both unit tests and subsystem tests.

- Integration testing — This is the best situation. Reexecute unit, subsystem, and integration tests.

Tactic 58

Jump on the Process Improvement Bandwagon

Before you institute a process improvement program, be sure you understand your goal. If your goal is to get a higher rating or to achieve compliance to some organizational standard, great! An example of a defective goal would be to improve the quality of your delivered software. That thought should send chills down your spine.

- To get the ball rolling, declare that the project will meet ISO9000 certification or reach some unattainable SEI/CMM level within six months. Choose a six-month period because the first four months will be wasted by your managers and staff simply hyping the effort.

- During the last two months apply pressure for something to be done, anything.

- When that doesn't occur, declare another period of process improvement—six months is again good—that will obviously be more productive because of all the ground work that was laid during the first period.

- Have your managers and staff generate presentations on the benefits of process improvement, write newsletter success story articles, go to conferences.

- Don't plan any doable intermediate milestones or hold your process improvement team to any schedule, because they might get the idea they're supposed to do something constructive.

Tactic 59

Create Lots of TQM Groups

Tomás de Torquemada, Spanish Grand Inquisitor, coined the buzzword TQM (Totally Quixotic* Methodology). Torquemada understood the inhuman pain necessary to achieve unwavering quality. His many disciples preserved his teachings, eventually settling in Japan. In the 1980's the revelation reached America, and a ground swell of faith spurred even the world's largest corporations to preach Torquemada's message of suffering.

Get everyone involved in DCA (Defects Cause Anguish) groups, from your department managers down to the lowliest programmer. The supplicants at each level should hold solemn, two-hour meetings at least twice a week to argue questions of doctrine. At the monthly convocation, have the leaders of these groups present their solutions to the world's problems. When the meeting ends, all join hands to sing the praises of TQM.

As their leader, praise these groups and vow to study their counsel in depth. Then chuck those papers and memos into the trash. Who do they think they're dealing with, anyway?

---

* 100 years after Torquemada, Miguel de Cervantes based his hero on this methodology.

Tactic 60

Hire a TQM Expert from outside the Company

Advertise for TQM experts, and your e-mail and snail mail inboxes will overflow with management wannabees. After careful consideration of all applicants, interview and hire the one who will make the most negative impact on your project. You can determine this through clever questions phrased to confuse the applicant:

1. "Name three companies with successful TQM programs." (There are none—this is a trick question.)

2. "Please *quantify* the results of TQM on your last job." (After a painful silence lasting a full minute, go on to the last question.)

3. "From what you've seen so far, how would you improve our TQM program?" ("Abolish it" is not a correct answer.)

Pick the candidate who

- Makes up three fictitious companies to answer question 1.

- Refers you to articles in the *Confessions of Software Engineering* to answer question 2.

- Sidesteps question 3 by asking you to define the word "improve."

74

Chapter 4

Morale Busters

The most important ingredient for project success is high team morale. It follows then that if you can destroy the morale of your development team, you stand an excellent chance to hurt the project badly.

Developers accept, and even enjoy, technical problems. They'll work late hours without pay to solve a particularly juicy design or coding problem, but if you wreck their morale, not even the most exciting technical problem will motivate them to succeed.

In the morale-destroying tactics presented here, the prime ingredient is convincing the employees that you consider them lower than dirt. This sounds deceptively easy, but most employees, especially those employees who have been with the company for several years, develop an innate company loyalty. They want desperately to believe that you care about their day-to-day well-being and that the company has their long-term interests at heart.

It's your job to shatter those misconceptions and illusions. As you proceed on this course, you'll find that your own morale increases in inverse proportion to the decrease in your team's morale. At the end of the project your team will be thoroughly demotivated, but you'll be on top of the world, eagerly awaiting that promotion for a job well done.

Tactic 61

Manage from a Distance

Developers would love to have you stop by just to chat, to reinforce that warm, fuzzy feeling that you care enough to waste time with them.

Clearly, then, you have to keep your distance from your team. The ultimate opportunity to distance yourself from your team comes during the last weeks before a major milestone or delivery to System Test. Go on a Caribbean cruise, or jet off to Hawaii or Europe for a well-deserved vacation. This will set an excellent example for all your managers.

On a more mundane day-to-day basis, use the following dodges:

- Advertise an open-door policy, but whenever anyone tries to exercise it, grant him five minutes, and when he sits down, ask him to prove he works for you. If at all possible, mispronounce his name. At the end of the five minutes, usher him out of your office with bogus promises that you'll address his concerns.

- Only show up at a developer's office when you have a problem he needs to fix or when it's time to do his performance appraisal (see Tactic 73).

- Wear custom-made $1,000 Italian suits and let developers know that you expect them to adhere to a professional dress code.

- Stride around with your jacket draped over your shoulders like an emperor's cape. This reinforces the idea that you think you are better than your underlings (Well, you are.).

- Hold a three-day management "retreat" (Atlantic City and Las Vegas are excellent host cities) to discuss project "strategy."

- Tell your employees that the company can no longer afford to subsidize the coffee fund.

Tactic 62

Let the Client Call the Shots

Letting the client call the shots occurs naturally when you have implemented Tactic 61. The major requirement for this perverse relationship to flower fully is for your team to be physically closer to the client than to you. If possible, place them in the same building as the client. Then if you aren't around to call the shots, the client will step in to fill the void, with predictable results—if the client could have done the job in the first place, he never would have hired your company.

This tactic can result in bizarre attempts at greater control by the client, such as establishing overly strict but useless design and coding conventions that will drive your developers to distraction (see also Tactic 15 and Tactic 27). However, the client will have that warm, fuzzy feeling because he is at the helm, even if the rudder is broken. You might even consider letting the client interview all new employees. It makes the client happy and simultaneously lets the new employee know who is in charge from the beginning.

Client control also has the distinct advantage that your people will feel abandoned. Whenever you stop by, reinforce this impression by strategically forgetting the names of two or three developers.

Tactic 63

Delegate Responsibility, Not Authority

This is so obvious that it shouldn't require discussion. However, the clever manager can implement this tactic in a manner guaranteed to rankle instead of merely to discourage:

- Tell your managers that they have complete authority over their own subsystem development, then casually overrule their decisions.

- Allocate insufficient office space to your managers' teams, then tell your managers it's up to them to find more.

- Never delegate authority for promotion and salary decisions. You can ask for promotion and salary recommendations from your managers. Always ignore those recommendations.

- Get your managers all excited by asking them to share their thoughts at important meetings, then ridicule them for proposing such stupid ideas.

Tactic 64

Establish a One-Way Professional Atmosphere

Instill in your managers and developers the following definition of a professional:

- Works more than 40 hours without expecting additional compensation.

- Places the needs of the company above any personal needs. So what if his wife is delivering a baby or his daughter is graduating from college? The build must go on.

- Works when he is sick, even if it kills him. The exact moment of death will be difficult to determine because he's already brain dead.

- Never takes a vacation, because he is too busy. This results in him losing accumulated vacation hours because he's over the maximum carryover.

- Never criticizes the company or management.

Tactic 65

Disregard Developers' Ideas for Improving Productivity

A particularly effective trick to play on developers is to hold one or more all-hands meetings to ask your team members for their ideas on improving productivity and addressing morale problems.

- Managers from other projects or HR (Heartless Resources) representatives should facilitate these meetings. This lends the semblance of sincerity.

- The facilitators should be sympathetic to the problems broached by the developers. Phrases like "I can't believe that's happening" and "Corporate will want to hear about this" are useful.

- Facilitators should emphasize that anonymity will be strictly maintained. When anyone asks why they are recording the names of developers who raise issues, facilitators should reply that it is purely for subsequent feedback on the resolution of the problems. These detailed notes by the facilitators will allow you to identify troublemakers in the future.

- Immediately after the meetings, issue a memo that "management" is investigating the issues raised and in the near future will be instituting sweeping changes to improve the work environment and productivity.

- Toss the minutes into a file drawer and forget about them.

Tactic 66

Institute Shift Work

When the development computer finally begins grinding to an almost complete stop between 10:00 AM and 5:00 PM, your team will bitch and moan. Instead of solving the problem (slow communications lines, not enough RAM, too many people running xclock, etc.), institute shift work. Split your team into three overlapping shifts: 8:00 AM - 5:00 PM, 4:00 PM - 1:00 AM, Midnight - 9:00 AM. Be sure to rotate workers on the shifts. Scientists have proven that rotating shifts create the most havoc in a worker's psyche.

The rationale for shift work is that most developers are not morning people (Test: how many are at work at 8:00 AM?). Instead, they thrive at night. They're used to staying up until the wee hours cranking out code at the last minute to complete their school projects. They'll thank you for the opportunity to return to the fond memories they had of undergraduate life in the dorms.

Tactic 67

Claim Low Productivity Results from Idle Developers

Your team has been working extra hours to finish the build. Four marriages are on the rocks (for this build only— the record is seven, for the previous build). It's time to apply a little pressure.

Hold an all-hands meeting to discuss poor productivity and lay the blame at the feet of the developers, who are

- Wasting too much time on the phone (probably telling their significant others that they won't be able to come home for dinner, breakfast, or the weekend).

- Holding too many meetings in the hallway to discuss non-work-related topics.

- Taking too many breaks.

- Spending too much time designing and coding simple functions (like that brain surgery simulator).

- Using resources improperly after normal business hours (a five-minute solitaire game at 2:00 AM is an unacceptable respite from coding).

Tactic 68

Require Overtime Work without Compensation

Developers have an extraordinary tendency to work overtime to get a job done without being asked. You'll find them going home at 6:00 PM and coming back just before midnight, then staying until 2:00 or 3:00 AM.

In any other industry this would be grounds for examining a worker's mental capacity. When was the last time your automotive technician said he was going to do some extra work on your Toyota for free?

This strange practice of developers results from a misguided pride in their work. How do you combat this unusual, and potentially successful behavior? The most effective methods to alienate developers and reduce their tendency to work for free are to

- Institute *required* overtime without pay, at least another 10 hours per week. Suddenly they'll hate having to stay at the office. (Their pride has been hurt.)

- Force everyone to be at the office on Saturday or Sunday, whichever is the most disruptive to their lives. Hold the aforementioned daily status meetings to ensure everyone works the entire day.

- Hire temp programmers who get paid for every hour they put on their time sheets (see **Tactic 70**).

Tactic 69

Ask Overburdened Developers to Work Proposals

The schedule is impossible, the client is enraged at the project's failure to meet milestones, response time is in the two-minute range, the developers are struggling to build the system by working 70-hour weeks—must be about time to start a proposal effort.

- Select a senior developer who is already wearing multiple hats as the chief designer, the code lead, and working on two or three TQM teams.

- Tell him on a Friday afternoon that, as the only qualified person (that'll make him feel good for a few moments), he's been chosen to work on the latest proposal.

- Assign him a section he knows nothing about.

- Give him an impossible schedule, e.g., first-cut draft due Monday SOB (Start of Bullshit). Try not to laugh when you express your regret that he has to work the one weekend he had freed up to get married and fly to Rio.

- When he drags himself in on Monday with a respectable contribution, give him another section due COB (Close of Bullshit).

- Continue this process until his wife-to-be deserts him. This may not work if she is also on your project, but then you should be giving her proposal assignments too.

Tactic 70

Hire Temp Programmers

When work starts to fall behind, hire several programmers from temporary agencies. Before long, your regular employees will quit to become temps also.

- Pay temps at least twice as much as your team members. After all, they don't get medical and other benefits, which are worth about 20% to 30% to your regular employees.

- Encourage temps to brag about how much money they make. If none of them will do this (an unlikely event), leak the information to your people.

- Pay temps for every hour (you have to anyway) and make your regular employees work extra hours without compensation (see Tactic 68). This fosters resentment between the temps and the regular employees.

- Give the temps career-enhancing jobs requiring new technology and make your regular employees do the uninteresting work.

Tactic 71

Supply Minimum Training and Conference Opportunities

As with most perks, allocating training and conference opportunities to just a few individuals is the best approach.

- Send one of your developers to training and to conferences so he can improve his resume and network into a better job.

    - When he quits, tell other employees that you don't train or send people to conferences because they'll just leave like the last person.

- Select a few employees to author papers recycled from their old papers, and let them write on company time.

    - This will impress the client and upper level management with your team's ability to generate publishable papers.

    - A side benefit is that developers too busy to write papers become disgusted with favoritism within the system.

- The people you select to write the papers should be those who can't do anything but write papers.

    - No development manager wants these employees because they are so theoretical they never get any real work done. If you assign them to development teams, they have a negative impact because they always want to design the software in the most complicated manner.

    - The best solution is to make them technical leads so they can screw up the design and still have time to write papers.

Tactic 72

Give Everyone the Same Bonus

This tactic works wonders for killing morale after your team successfully completes a tough milestone:

- During development, raise expectations of lucrative bonuses based on individual contribution to the effort. Throw around figures in the hundreds of thousands or millions of dollars to generate excitement.

- When it's time to distribute the bonuses, include people who didn't have anything to do with making the milestone—try to double or triple the number of recipients to bring down the average bonus. If you include the temp programmers, you can generate unprecedented animosity between the regulars and the temps.

- Give everyone the same, small bonus—whether a new hire or a battle-scarred veteran—except for those people who worked multiple 70-hour weeks to meet the milestone. Give them an additional $50 or $100 as a slap in the face to wake them up and guarantee they won't bust their butts again for the project.

- Always use this approach on an early milestone. Once you have disappointed the developers, promises of fantastic bonuses for later milestones will fall on jaded ears.

Tactic 73

Give Humiliating Performance Reviews

Employees anticipate performance reviews with mixed emotions. They hate doing the paperwork, but it's the one chance they get every year to toot their own horns. Show them how important they are to you:

<u>Preparation:</u>

- Tell the developer you need his input immediately, then procrastinate and eventually hold the review meeting several months later than scheduled.

- Delegate your part of the appraisal to a lower-level manager who has no idea what the developer has been doing for the last year.

<u>The Meeting:</u>

- Hold the meeting in your office, where you can intimidate the developer from behind your desk. You might also consider a glass-walled conference room so that everyone can watch your victim cry.

- Give your comments (which all levels of management have already approved) to the developer real-time (maximum 5-minute meeting) so he has no chance to evaluate your comments and prepare his defense.

- Welcome interruptions of the meeting to let the developer know you could be doing *important* work.

- An alternate approach is to slip the appraisal under the developer's door at night and *never* hold the review meeting.

Content:

- Belittle the developer's accomplishments but lavishly praise his peers.

- Focus on a trivial mistake the developer made six months ago.

- Overload the developer with unattainable goals for the next review.

Tactic 74

Get Rid of Developers over 40

Your best workers are probably those developers over 40 years old because they have the experience and the judgment to do the job correctly. However, they are also more expensive in terms of salary and benefits, resulting in a lower profit margin. You need to get rid of them. Yes, it's illegal to discriminate against workers over 40, but here are several ways to achieve the same result without incurring the wrath of the Justice Department:

- When work comes along that requires a new language or tool, require six months' paid experience in the skill. Then you can tell older employees who apply that they don't meet the qualifications for the position, whether or not they could learn what they need in a few weeks.

- Tell older workers that the company is overstaffed. Suggest they find other positions before the big layoff.

- Lay off older workers for lack of work; then hire IROCs a month later to fill the unanticipated job openings.

- Hire self-proclaimed hot-shot IROCs, make them leads, and encourage them to squeeze more work out of older employees. Another welcome result of this strategy is that the IROCs won't always be questioning your management and technical judgment like more experienced developers.

Tactic 75

Refer to People as "Units"

Hold an All-Hands meeting to discuss company woes and the lack of new business. Casually mention that so many "units" will be let go from some organization—the project, the division, the company, it doesn't matter. What's important is that employees begin to feel that they are disposable. A particularly effective approach is to have someone from HR, supposedly the protectors of employee interests, give the speech. Your employees already know not to trust their own management, and now they'll learn that no one in the company cares about them.

A few days after the meeting bring in some new, expensive hire, such as a TQM consultant (see Tactic 60) to show employees what is really important to management.

Tactic 76

Tie Promotions to Involvement in Process Improvement

If you've done your job correctly, your employees should now cringe at the mention of SEI, CMM, SCE, ISO9000 or TQM. To bring it all home, you must tie promotions to an employee's involvement in process improvement activities:

- Add process improvement activities as a special section on performance review forms.

- Proclaim that no employee will be promoted without significant involvement in process improvement. This will result in employees joining multiple TQM groups to impress management, thereby decreasing time spent on development.

First-line managers will become frustrated when they can't promote based on technical merit. Eventually they knuckle under and waste time generating memos that exaggerate or invent process improvement efforts by their people.

To further torque these managers and unpromoted employees, every once in a while promote some truly incompetent individual to a senior management or staff position just to see who quits.

Tactic 77

Keep the Stockholders Happy

The best way to keep stockholders happy is to maximize profits and minimize expenditures, so you have to stop paying those developers so much:

- Tell your employees that the company is doing badly. Ignore published reports in *The Wall Street Journal* that the company has just experienced its best quarter in 30 years.

- Declare that a 2% raise should be considered an exceptional raise this year.

- Cut medical and other benefits and make the employees pay more for them. Employees are accustomed to deceptive packaging at the grocery store, so they should not be surprised to have this happen at work.

- Ask developers to commit to a 50-hour workweek (also see Tactic 68) to bring down the rates that you bid for new work.

These maneuvers have an added benefit: good developers will leave for better salaries, and *you are the person* who made them more desirable to other companies by keeping their salaries low! Eighty percent of those who stay will be the ineffective developers who are afraid to leave or the IROCs you bid per Tactic 4. The effect on your project will be drastic both in terms of quality and schedule. Congratulations, you sly fox.

List of Acronyms

BDR — Build Disaster Review

CASE — Completely Autistic Software Engineering (tools)

CDR — Comical Design Review

CM — Chaos Management

CMM — Completely Meaningless Model

COB — Close of Bullshit

COTS — Constantly Ordering the Sequel

DCA — Defects Cause Anguish

DDS — Detailed Disaster Specification

DSI — Dubious Source Instructions

GUI — Generally Useless Interface

HR — Heartless Resources

IDE — Impractical Development Environment

IROC — Idiot Right out of College

ISO — In Search of

KSLOC — Killer SLOC

LCD — Least Capable or Logic-Challenged Developer

NIH — Not-Invented-Here

OO — Object-Oriented; Obscure on-purpose

OOD — OO Disaster

PAO — Project Aggravation Office

PDL — Program Divining Language

PDR — Preliminary Disaster Review

PDS   — Preliminary Disaster Specification

QA   — Quantity Assurance

RFP   — Request for Puffery

SCE   — Software Comedy Evaluation

SEI   — Software Exhibition Institute

SEN   — Software Engineering Nostrum

SLOC   — Shifting Lines of Code

SOB   — Start of Bullshit

SRR   — Senseless Requirements Review

SRS   — Senseless Requirements Specification

TQM   — Totally Quixotic Methodology

VCR   — Vast Corporate Resources

WAG   — Wild-Assed Guess

Index